Lone Dog's
Winter Count

Diane Glancy

West End Press

Now compare our gifts of prudence, talent, magnanimity, temperance, humanity, & religion with those little men (homunculos) [the Indian] *in whom you will scarcely find traces of humanity; who not only lack culture but do not even know how to write, who keep no records of their history except certain obscure and vague reminiscences of some things put down in certain pictures . . .*
—Juan Gínes de Sepúlveda
Valladolid, Spain, circa 1550

Acknowledgment to *Oxford Magazine* for "Sandstone Rock in Your Hand"; *Seneca Review* for "Spinning in Space" and "A Single Row of Pines"; *Timbuktu* for "Portrait of Lone Dog"; *National Poetry Competition Anthology* (Chester Jones Foundation) for "Manly Heart"; *The American Voice* for "Portrait of the Disguise Artist"; *Negative Capability* for "The First Reader"; *Nimrod* for "Death Cry for the Language"; *Sow's Ear* for "E Wa Coo Me's Conversion"; *Calyx* for "Trying to Crow"; *Permafrost* (University of Alaska) for "Truck Stop on Highway 80 Near Walcott, Iowa"; *Black River Review* for "Hamatawk"; *The Journal* (Ohio State University) for "Lone Dog's Winter Count"; *Oklahoma Review* for "The Pack-Up" and "After the Thaw"; *Mid-America Review* (Bowling Green University) for "Yeast"; *Hayden's Ferry Review* (Arizona State University) for "Homework"; *Red Dirt* for "White Words You Can Hardly See," "Untitled," and "Portrait of the Escape Artist"; and *Little Magazine* for "Here I Am Standing by Myself" and "Overpass."

Grateful acknowledgment to the Equal Opportunity Fellowship and the Edwin Ford Piper Fellowship, University of Iowa, and to the Frances C. Allen Fellowship from the D'Arcy McNickle Center for the American Indian at the Newberry Library, Chicago, which made this manuscript possible.

First edition, November 1991
ISBN 0-931122-64-3
$9.95

The reproduction of the Buffalo Robe on the cover ("Lone Dog's Winter Count") is by permission of the Newberry Library in Chicago.

Book design by Michael Reed
Typography by Prototype

West End Press • P.O. Box 27334 • Albuquerque, NM 87125

Contents

I

Here I Am Standing Beside Myself 2
This-Is-Where-We-Go-On-Winter 3
Homework 4
Coyote's Volvo 5
Portrait of the Escape Artist 6
Truck Stop on Highway 80 near Walcott, Iowa 7
Unbuttered 8
An End to Drought 9
Overpass 10

II

Lone Dog's Winter Count 12
Etude for Tuba 14
Manly Heart 16
Arcane 17

III

Iowa: Volcano 20
Yeast 21
Invocation 22
Hamatawk 23
Sandstone Rock in Your Hand 24
E Wa Coo Me's Conversion 25
The Road Paved to Heaven 26
She Was Spinning in Space 27
A Single Row of Pines 28

IV

Trying to Crow 30

V

The First Reader 36
The White Farm 37
White Words You Can Hardly See Against the Sky 38
Portrait of the Disguise Artist 39
Kemo Sabe 40

Portrait of the Artist as Indian 41
Lone Dog 42
The Imaginary Indian 43

VI

Death Cry for the Language 46

VII

Portrait of the Lone Survivor 58
Untitled 61

VIII

Portrait of the Sufficiency of Winter 64
Portrait of Lone Dog 65
February 10, Late Afternoon 66
Late Winter 67
After the Thaw 68
The Pack-Up 69
ti:ki:tuhu'i 70
Portrait of Spring 71
A Gesture to the Sky 72
Just After 73

Notes

Lone Dog's Winter Count 77

For Gerald Stern
and Alvin Greenberg
who opened doors for me

I

HERE I AM STANDING BESIDE MYSELF

Just look at the family album. My white mother
her sisters their husbands our cousins. Then my
father my brother & I the stuffed skin of sparrow
hawks on our heads the *g'ig'ig'ig'ig'i* in our
throats.

My father said his grandfather fled Indian
Territory *kuna' yeli st'di* [claw-scratch-like]
when he'd done something wrong. We were outcast
now as well as Indian. & only part of them.
Outcast of outcasts. *ju!jiji skew!* It was a
sense I had. I'm trying to find the words.

It's when I remember the taste of cornbread soaked
in squirrel-grease. The feeling we weren't but
really were. The Cherokee hymns I heard in brush-
arbors. The corn-god Jesus at festival hops.

It's when I see the moon is male. Vigilant &
traveling at night. [Now cast some beads around
the neck of your wife the sun & wrap her in weasel-
skin & darken her face so the clouds will come.]

It's when I remember the raccoon turtle deer that
nibbled at my feet at night. I still hold my legs
up to myself pull my fingers insideout draw my
arms into my chest my ears & nose into my head.

THIS-IS-WHERE-WE-GO-ON-WINTER

We're supposed to praise his name but I feel anger over the birth of the Christ-life within. I walk down the country road, turn back into the wind. This land was ours, now we should forgive the fields snapped with fences & power lines? Under the cloud-bank, a new cornfield shines in the sun like ripples on a lake. Now the road cuts into a hill, the dirt packed like old cement on a cellar floor. When the rain begins to fall, I shiver & know the wind plants a cold in my chest like a row of beans. Later when I talk, I hear a voice which is not mine. An ancestor when he was old & sick & had one foot in the next county. I'm supposed to praise his name? Lord God of bitterness & defeat, the cold rips out the throat, head, chest, leaving green sprouts of healing, the new vision quest.

HOMEWORK

Years later you dream 2 birds fly across the road, one eating the other. Even then you dreamed your father took your brother to the barber shop to cut off his head. The packing house, I guess. Slaughter was always with us. I smelled it when he drove his Willis in the garage at night. His unnotched belt was something you didn't take ahold of. But she marked with clock-marks, the hands passing minutes over her face as she rushed you up the hill to school. Pushed to church. The time comes to say you're moving on. The stockyards close down. The pretty aunt dies of cancer, her jaw, half her face eaten away. Then his body goes, finally, hers. But in church there's a leap to the resurrection, a cord of faith that pulls you through. Like the jars of intestinal worms he brought from the stockyards for you to take to science. Right up the ramp to the kill.

COYOTE'S VOLVO

A freeze-rain & Coyote slides over the road! His Volvo separates
from its front fender on a guardrail. He gets out, kicks the ass
of his car. He curses the grease-job of the road. He curses the
sky which puckers like a dark brain or shriveled balls. His anger
blazes a barrel-fire beside the road. The chrome of his Volvo
caught in the trap of the rail! Broken glass, a bent tailpipe. Hah
rah kay mo. He rubs his hands & chants. The flames glitter on
ice. His ribbon jacket, refried jeans. A cowpunk bumper-sticker.
No one stops. Ho-po-te co-yo-te. His hairy toe sore from the
swift kick to the Volvo. Making loVvo to his oVvol. A passerby
yells, there's a law against leashless coyotes. He looks to the
hard sky over him, the leaderless stars. Now he is Co-yoyo-te,
shivering herder of wooly ashes when he stirs the barrel-fire.
Hoombago. War Man from Walmart. His binoculars, field cam-
eras, his fur slick as congoleum.

PORTRAIT OF THE ESCAPE ARTIST

The fields with their markings. The cornshocks
of wickiups. A heave of smokeholes

squirting out cornfields.
My father loaded with duck & rabbit.

The steam of their skinned bodies in the cold.
Coiled intestines like words I said

but my voice reached neither ear.
My brother with the duck-call. How we laughed.

I'd hear him under the covers after the lights were out.
Quack. We heard the warning from the other room.

But he quacked & he quacked again beneath the beating.
He'd wheeze between breaths while I gathered

pieces of his bones the pearls of
broken strings they rolled across the floor

under fields the light weightness of them.
The heavens coming out from under their lid.

TRUCK STOP ON HIGHWAY 80 NEAR WALCOTT, IOWA

A mechanic opens the hood of my car, shows me how the fan wobbles because the water pump has gone bad. The man, I'm amazed, knows everything. He tells me about the car I've driven 155,000 miles, as if he'd been in it for 10 years, as if his hands touched the wheel. The air & light sparkle in the grease & trucks roar like mammoths. I ask if I can drive to Chicago & he says I can't drive across the street. The fan would go through the radiator & blackness would enfold me like a tunnel. He separates the radiator from its fan, removes the hose. Inside the truckers talk to waitresses, looking at road signs to remember where they are. Some woman hangs a cigarette from her mouth. A man at the table coughs while he eats. 2 hours lost on the road while the mechanic replaces the water pump in my car. Then the hose is connected to the engine again & the hood closed. How many generations have we walked this leaking edge of the road? The thought of Chicago, its lake shore always moving, as if near death when one sees those already in the next world & hears the chanting from the sacred ground.

UNBUTTERED

To say it well or else not say what happens,
the pearl onions in a bucket
not everything
but a part. Spit it when you can, dear.
The years of land-run in perpetual motion.
On the horizon a slender hawk,
the battery of light.
Focus one tongue
the wagon wheels follow.
A kitchen table over linoleum,
you'd think it was buried under the years
circling back upon itself.
But a toaster pops
the flick of a tin fish
& you see it rise again,
not the whole but a slice of it
still warm.
The window curtains
a plain which is distress to the claws of memory.
Swiftly dear, retrieve what you can
suck it, pry it loose, not with your finger
but a butter knife, the burnt smell
rising now.

AN END TO DROUGHT

Open the field under the mower,
find where to climb out.
Clubber the sides of the will,
take your own hand again.
SPEAK to yourself.
Crawl out from feelings
burned off like fields.
Hold the AIR in your cupped hand,
say to the emptiness it is SOMETHING,
say it is water.
Say it until a cloud crowds the sky.
Let the rain fill your cupped hand,
DRINK until you are full.
Drink until you say
it is air.

OVERPASS

Suddenly there's a shot like the sound of a cavalry cannon. We wobble to the side of the overpass & find a tire blew. There's not much room. The viaduct vibrates when trucks pass. My son says people die like this. The car moves back on the jack when the rear wheels lift off the ground. I push against the car to keep it from falling off the jack. The Great Spirit wearing a buffalo hat & sacred lizard paint holds the car with me. Grit & dust gall the evening sun, making petroglyphs of the tire on its post, bolts holding it in place. I nail the antelope to the cave wall, the expressway an animal-hunt now our space pushing toward the distant hunting ground. As if on a body-cast the tire, the smoking blowout, the rim digging into the sky. Then a viaduct over the railroad tracks, a river beside the train.

II

*. . . it is lawfull & necessarye to trade & traficke with
the Savages . . . & further that the Christians may
travaile into those Countries & abide there whome the
Savages may not justly impugne & forbidde in respect of
mutuall society & fellowship between man & man
prescribed by the Law of Nations.*

*For from the first beginning of creation of the world &
from the renuing of the same after Noes floode, all men
have agreed, that no violence shoulde be offered
Ambassadours. That the Sea with his Havens shoulde
bee common . . . & that Strangers shoulde not be dryven
away from the place of Countrey whereunto they doo come.*
—George Peckum in his treatise justifying English
colonization of the New World

LONE DOG'S WINTER COUNT

1.

The dread waking with him nudging his ear.

He knew the split-dream   filled afterwards
(cornfields.) *Ki ye*. But in that then,
that present in moment of geese-flying grasses-moving,
time lay under the doom-sense he woke with.

Upshore a new sky, new stress points. The burial ground
of stars burning nightly.

Lone Dog looked for the-pulled-beyond not blacked-out
by the NOW.

Hei yow. More than was in the land before him
the Spirit squatting like a dull chief picking
the cold sores on his nose.

Why the wind change? Why wind?

Was there a motion of trees to carry them through?
This way (not that). The nothing that could be done.
Their canoes pushing the river forward
the hooves of horses smoothing grasses where they passed.

2.

Ki yop the dread on all of them now.
The tribe asking what he saw what he knew.
He thought of them like a single wanting.

It was another spirit taking the land wiping out
different ways at once.

Lone Dog sat at the council fire watched its edges eat
the air like prairie fire in grass.

Often he flinched as though an arrow pierced his body
often he reached for breath.

He knew their legends knew their words of strength
he had always heard.

But now Lone Dog was pushed into dry land.
He remembered how it had been
the words left of it anyway in the tiny womb of the ear.

3.

Now wind hurries the river.
The snow nestling their fingers.

The tribe waits for the voice of Lone Dog to pierce the silence
to father thought
like children running into their heads.

Let go of the baggage
let go of the dogs with their packs of small hides
& beading needles.

Everywhere snow whirls into the crevice of the tribe
hurling their massive wandering into the empty hole
of their bellies.

He sees a dead woman
the edge of her blanket moving
as though her hand under it still scraped hides.

4.

The cold drives the heat of the body toward the heart
away from the toes & fingers the outer rim of the ears
the tip of the nose up the arms & legs trying.

There is a hunger that gnaws the head until it is
light & dizzy.

Then the warm little heart alone in the chest
calls the will in to dream with it
one last time before going.

ETUDE FOR TUBA

1.

It was a leap forward for them.
Their ignorance had to be wakened.
Another form of life came & they were mowed under.

They had to recognize it.
I showed them my garden after frost,
the dried & brittle flowers.
I held them under the skritch of evening along the ground.

What were they? Savages on the plains!
Now they are evangelized.

Ah yes, they believed in a Great Spirit. But what
did they know? They hadn't been tried.

They hadn't scalded in the prairie sun.
Now they they have eyes like us. They see God through Christ
our Lord.

It's worth it to lose one's way of life if at the end
one sees God?

2.

At first there were no windows.
The birds flew above us during mass. Finally,
wagons arrived with crates of the Saints.
Christ in his magnificence. Mary John Peter.

Ah! this barren land. The Indian with his arms
outflung to fields. The crucified, cross-shaped church
in his image.

No other form bears the weight you know
of limbs frozen in snow.
Fingers gnawed by rodents

& raunchy Mary in her gaudy gown
the Medea-gift of a gold robe with fillets of poison.

Blankets with smallpox hidden as a small gift
a thorn in their forehead to be picked out
they died as Glauce screaming in agony.

The first frost of the soul
the flecked virgin all of her pantywaists in her flock.

Let's clutter them with icons
they'll never find their way
argue among ourselves the Baptists & Catholic priests

The virgin giggling behind her bouquet of bluets.

3.

The division of sound ruptured the task passed through.
Wind in a sudden cornfield.

Its increase of subtleties. Someone (Christ) had to die.
Now it's the Indian.

The tuba section (precious one)
sunk into the yesterday of the first part.

At first they thought the world was a black wool blanket
an outbreak of October maples (red deer, mid-air).
Dying winters in a thin succession on the ration line.

The stars were yard lights in the gracious catalogue.
They could say Christ
the aftermath of high prairie he gave.

MANLY HEART

Flat Warclub remembered. Yes, there had
been rumor that a band living at Blue Mounds
had what was known as a manly-hearted woman.
—Frederick Manfred, *The Manly-Hearted Woman*

I had a vision of a marsh hawk dropping through the air. I found a feather by my feet & kept it in a medicine bundle. After the vision, I dressed like a man. My time in the woman's-lodge ceased. I took a wife who sewed a buffalo suit & head for me. When a brave stampeded a herd of buffalo toward the cliff, my arrow went into a bull's neck. On long hunts I thought of my wife. How she carried wood & water, scraping her fingers, burning her neck with the strips of buffalo sinew. How she warmed the robes at night, told stories to the orphans in camp in her foxskin shawl. Soon I saw as many long-hair soldiers as there had been buffalo. I saw the marsh hawk dropping through the air again. I knew it was a vision of defeat. I trusted the ghost shirt my wife made & the soldiers' bullets went by. When we were without enough black powder, I could see the ball going through the air from my musket. Then a grease-soldier killed my wife in a cavalry raid. I combed her hair with a buffalo tongue, sacrificed 2 dogs for her, 1 to eat on the long trip to the hunting grounds & the other for a guide. My knife slit their throats quickly, spilling blood into the little trough I made. Now I wear my wife's beadwork with my medicine bundle. My tribe flees the soldiers closing in behind us. In my vision, the marsh hawk is not able to open its wings. The tribe becomes thin as a shadow one follows from this world. Now I am like the feather in my medicine bundle.

ARCANE

Ah! He heard the story in English from Reverend Bushyhead. The man who made a canoe only it was an ark & he brought the animals 2 by 2, the wolverines, the buffalo, the whooping cranes, crows, beaver, bear, prairie dog, & shut them up in stalls because the Great Spirit told him to. & he sat in the canoe with his squaw & his sons & their squaws & the Great Spirit made thunder which they had not heard before. It was the growl of a huge winged bird, the stampede of buffalo hooves across the prairie. It was a word echoing back into itself the way he could yell into an empty reservation room & hear his voice as though it were a herd of language.

Now he heard the animals closed in the ark. He heard the man spearing hay into their stalls. Finally he got to hear the story again in the church on the reservation. Reverend Bushyhead wouldn't tell it all the time like he asked. But now the sky flashed with light as though another moon were born. A crash & then a flash again. The squaws whimpered. They heard water not like a river or stream nor even water poured from a storage pot, but water broken into pieces like words. Rain. *Ya hoy ay ho!* That was it!

Now he wore a sign on his back, I speak Cherokee. He wore it in the classrooms & study hall. He wore it in the mess hall & dormitory. At night when he slept the sign rubbed his shoulders. At times the string gripped his neck. The sign tried to take his breath the way the schoolmaster tried to take his words. He could not speak his own language. It was forbidden. How like warriors his fingers were folded on the desk, naked & bent in their shallow graves. How like featherless crows. Now the flood of silence. He gathered his words into the closed canoe. 2 by 2. The words shut up in his throat & the sounds they made far down in his heart.

III

IOWA: VOLCANO

You walk the field
as if over a crackling leaf fire.
You hear the whoop of it
up through tunnels of roots,
the countless holes & fissures
of stalks in the soil.
The Spirit seeps into the given world.
You feel it between slices
of the spruce.
Indominate
the glad yellowing of earth,
the sidestep of raking
all other leaves.
The hard force of them to stop the car.
You thong the back of the old garage
shed really
jarring the sudden lava beds,
children jumping
through smoke of eraser dust,
crows erupting from cornshocks
on an autumn day.

YEAST

I fear the dark will disappear.
I set out sticky stars,
wire them for constant light.
I rake a few brown leaves for a pile,
board up the sky against the sun.
I drop water on my breadboard for a flood,
imagine chickens floating by on rooftops,
I throw them grain.
After a while I sweep the floodwaters with my broom.
I form a house,
a yard.
A flock of birds chirp under the bush near the feeder
the faded sheets flap on the line.
I form a dog barking,
the children,
a husband with his fist inched above us.

INVOCATION

You bend the road where light begins,
watcher of cock fights
& pearls on the ears of loud women.
You plow chaos
with your tractor
& pull from me the teeth of gladness.
You are the image of stars,
the whisper of wind on a county road.
Under our flooring
there's mud like lard in cake pans.
You, God, squatting in your tomato-
rows, would you look up?
There's a massacre going on,
we're fast turning the last corner we can turn.
We're calling out your name.
E hok a yee. You Spirit,
in our harness
we believe.

HAMATAWK

Just it was (crow tongued) he was saying a caw.
Then wings fold up the Indian
if antlers deer give up
totems of the head the anyhow of them.
This coat gets smaller each year
like the tepee I came from
when I (back) to the (space) I was born,
the small hohum of it,
old ones all reversed
smaller the autumn trees than I remember
(the way) old language breaks.
Hum way to hum hum the buzzled wiggle
of the tall grasses smoothed down
by the path of them (to woods) through the field.
I'm going & if not
I come back smaller.
Then he (the crow) sings like this
his mouth he opens. Caw. Caw. The grasses
(wave) they take flight the crow wings (grasses
burnt) all fields shrivel
next the new world.

SANDSTONE ROCK IN YOUR HAND

Was it rain that left a hole,
not clear through, but deep at one end?
A cockpit when you flew the rock
looking for a place to land
just before sleep closed its gate,
& you had to find a field or runway
in the first strip of light?
Or the vacancy in the porous rock
was the open trunk of the car
when you unloaded packages?
A saguaro with a bird's nest in its arm
where you went for the holidays?
No, it was more like the space
between you & your brother
in the backseat when the gray road
went by. You try to wipe the windshield
because instrument flight
fights against instinct.
You reach back for the land you left
in sleep, but turnpike tickets spit
at you, the wipers frantic
& you don't know
if you're in the road or air.
Maybe *you* are that hole
rain has washed out. Your porous surface
didn't hold against the torrents
& torments of this low flight,
the hopelessness, the tunnel
not broken through.

E WA COO ME'S CONVERSION

She twirls & twirls
on the dance floor,
her skirt higher & higher
off the ground spinning round
& round first her knees show
then her thighs
soon the lace on her panties.
The skirt rises higher over her head.
It sucks her up into itself,
her shoulders waist hips knees
ankles her little red toes.
She dances inside her skirt.
The starch in her crinoline
twinkles like stars in the universe.
Ah! that's where she moves now,
the black space of herself where
all memories put on white faces,
ribbons hanging from the ears,
bright red spots on the cheeks.
They come alive & speak now,
their Bible open
the Saints pouring out
Paul Peter Mary Joseph Jesus.

THE ROAD PAVED TO HEAVEN

God is tuned in to us
his antennae turn to the speck of any
distant roar,
his thoughts move like the blue dot of tractor
in the field.
Tires tied over a tarp over a haymound,
that's where faith begins.
In the peepholes
I hear the pines
their clumps twerping near silos.
He believes we're here,
the angels put his finger on our corral.
You see the road's not really there
& you can't make it without him,
but if you believe it's there
it's there
& you transcend the slot of God
& you're in.

SHE WAS SPINNING IN SPACE

The little soul twirling
at last like a leaf on the sycamore,
her absolute level best.
Ah yes this was the turning that was squashed,
this was the life ripped from her
like the beginning of a feeling
that rises but was chopped.
& all the while longing to rise again,
to dance to say *ya sota* to the Spirit,
to speak his language,
to feel the pines beneath it.
The dancing bedrock the frilly edge of Timothy
& Johnson grass.
To weave back the separation the split in the head,
the braids released over her two feet dancing,
the blessed will of her passage
to mere space
with a wedge of certain life.
The pure drive to come from the back room
along the clear air enfolding the hall,
the sycamore leaves snake-dancing
on her lovely yellow dress.

A SINGLE ROW OF PINES

White farmhouse,
barn sheds enclosures of hounds
baying at the morning light,
the hanging of it inside your head.
It's where you drive into the country.
The harvester spitting dried stalks into the truck,
the one part giving into the other.
The finely drawn lines the backbreaking work
leaning over fields,
the pencil & ruler never taking your
eyes off the ground the stubblerows
of mowed cornstalks.
It's where
you find you left a part of yourself
in the kernels husks now invisible in the field,
the roots even a clean eye cannot see
despite the closely drawn lines,
the careful laying of plots.
Beloved rows & mowers of them this is where
the naked soul cries in its room,
come out now you have
numberless roads up the slope of cornland.
Trembling, weaklimbed,
after coaxing it sits at the feedstore
in the old stone Mississippi River blufftown.
You find a tomahawk in its head,
you pull it out with a thwarp.
Now your soul teeters a moment
until you steady it.
Its eyes unused to the hanging light,
the crash of yellow hillsides in October,
you say here put on this silver bonnet of a silo,
you say here.

IV

TRYING TO CROW

1. Cro(row)

The same was in the beginning. The whole here under
the branch.

The same landscape of half-light & shade
under the tree our ancestors walked the trail.
Their mouths move but there is no sound.

The God Spirit, the angels flying over the tribe.
Wa-tum-ka the crow-black hair a fence in the world.

I say Christ even pale-faced Christ the whole of being.
The-Whom-of-our-cultures who shoved into us
the nonetheless.

The same sky floats near the ceiling, the branches
in airspace over the wood floor.
We say caw we are on this margin, this pantry shelf.

Lo! In far space the stars fly from the cocoon moon.
Our tribe migrates to new territory.

Sometimes they look down as though we were the darkness
carried in a basket.

Sometimes we look up through the sky-holes & see
the braves in warbonnets, the warriors in feather bustles,
the Christ with his pony-drag cross.

2. Cro-de-loo

What's it like behind the orange shelf of evening sky? The stray
edge of a cornfield in those clouds there below? Is it speeding
over the hump of hill (leaving our seats as the car starts down)?
Is it the time we rode the ferris wheel (stopped at the top where
I screamed until I climbed the air)? What's it like not having the
ground under your feet? All summer the fields spread under
the eye. I feel the seed drop the breaking of shell the root & then
the stem pushing into light. Our past is in that vacuum of deso-
lation (the night rotting the head) until Christ pierced the eye
(lighted the dark). Not them who brought him, no, but the bitter
Christ their Lord.

3. Trying the Whad 4

Now there is sound
Whad the wurd
the whad du of it
The fledgling in the shade tree
feathers under its transparent wings
like straight-pins on a card
Iz the advent of the Tribe
Our feet bled in snow
We dund know whad happen
We hab to chalk-in the blanks
The trackts of corpzes grazing
heaving soundz
We not knowding whad they mean
Whez there ever a way
to say without wurds
Quick make of it
a window in the pantry of the room
Ground strikes the buffalo
topped by carbines
The gauze of wurdzah spins
huza huza
He conjugates our trail
The rags of his voice
a night lifted with a clunk.

4. Craw

We know their sacred wailing in the yoke
plowing furrows on their backs (taking the ruin
of the moon) so we could go into the new

trying to learn it all
as though a girl who asks how to spell a long word
leaving the paper on her desk
as if she could carry the letters in her head

as if we could carry it all
deliver it like the morning paper on the steps
(a Christmas tree dragged to the tipi)
(outside the dead bird the gray moon of its breast
no longer rising the 2 feet like antennae on the roof)
as though even a part of it could be told.

I thought what it was to be Indian.
What was left of what we were.
The corners of the earth folding up (here in the room).
God, Christ, the Holy Ghost & Christ's Bride
holding the corners saying give me your corner,
No, you take mine.
& God blowing his ref-whistle without giving a chance
to get into it.

Hail Christ killed & brought back to life
(near the shade tree) holding the trigger fingers
of soldiers & warriors in a cup.

5. Cro-nav-i-dos

Jesus was born under the blacK sKillet moon. Buf-
falo & Reindeer crossed the plains. The Mother
Mary wore a bucKsKin dress. Joseph had a Coyote-
sKin on his head. The presents were wrapped liKe
war axes. Mary held the sKeleton Baby on her bacK.
Behold the reaching fingers of her hands. The roc-
Ket Star above the Tree.

6. Vamoose

The reindeer with horns
trot through the woods
like priests carrying the Crucifix
Graveyards of stars cross the sky
The triumphant angels
their wings billowing like flour sacks
fly in formation
their headlights beaming on the road
first in line
they say He's here
yep
the Christ child
He's in Bethlehem
with animals
the bear
the porcupines
pigeons
all say stay with us Christ

At the church-rails for years to come
we pray for hallowed ground
stringing vertebrae
like popcorn
& cranberries
His ecstasy the last huzah

7. Papoose

The hangels triumfunt
because The Christ Baby sleeps
a Lamb in the manger
Wake up now
we need you in this duzbohl
the fist in line
to say the burdens lifted
our backs not bent with bundles
we carried to the new land in the cold
the wayzood
bells be glory to The Baby King
Tried-Star-of-Bethleme
grow up now quickly
claw the hollowed ground
rake the huzah
tear a hole
in the spasms of our spirit dance.

8. Cawing

Their arms too heavy for birds they'd flop on the ground
like us in the new territory

they say here the end of the trail now live
We say Great Spirit who made the Urth from nothing

make this land our fields cabins quilts language
The Spirit alone guides us

The ground reaches our toes up
It is here we first thought what are we?

The first row in the land
the narrow light from the moon in its tube?

The fields squawed & warriored.

The generator steaming with gizmos.

An American Flyer on the arc of the soccer system.
The warrior-part flothes in the universe.

The church reorganist plays Geons to the Christ.
Skeletons rise from churchyards.

The ghosts of rabbits, rodents, their bones
in bags of coyotes, the *wa wa* of the yet unknowable.

The crows pick up the guest-corner of fields,
twang a dust-trail 10 light-years wide.

Unfork the star map over the barley rows.
Magnetic storms water the peans, lentils.

The solar-pie here under the ceiling, over the wood floor.
The propane tank of a backyard torpedo.

V

. . . doleful creatures who were the veriest ruines of mankind, which were found on earth.
—Cotton Mather

THE FIRST READER
SANTEE TRAINING SCHOOL, 1873

It was insane. I thought it myself. The winter
count Sits-Down-By-Mistake drew, he said it was his
name, in the school he drew in books an antelope
with an arrow in his rump the white man screaming
we killed 3 of their men. They whacked his hands
& gave him other books to read. "This is a
sailboat. It looks nice on water. John is in
the boat. He knows how to steer." Sits said it
was especially significant to read a book on
sailing when his father prays for a bucket-full to
pour on his cornrow. He clung to my neck all day.
Worried about a ship's rigging & the waters
covering the land. There's a place where it's all
water. He knew it now. But there'd NEVER be
another flood. Remember our ancient stories? The
water we came through now trapped in our ear. He
drew water-lungs on the antelope so they could
breathe in water, made a generator that pumped the
land dry. They hit him again & taped his hands.
This is a little sailboat.
De sína watopekiyapi wata cistinna.
It looks nice on the water.
Mini akan owanyag wáste hinca.
John is in the boat.
John wata kin en yanka.
Is John afraid?
John kokipa he.
John knows how to steer the boat.
John iyupse yuza onspe.
When Sits read in his own tongue they taped it
shut in his mouth.

THE WHITE FARM

Old rabbit house, chicken pens, barn. The sun hissing in the trees; wind all over the place. Maple seeds with their hairy wings fly in a tailspin if you let them. In the meantime you measure your rhubarb. You have the pie dough precisely on the plate. You remember when you first heard the earth was round & you thought it was shaped like a pie. You knew it anyway by the tribe's migration back to the same place when you always knew you were headed straight. You remember your footsteps through the snow. The open chest of winter; lungs stiff as grocery sacks. The voice of sheep wake the air. You would forget to rise, stripping frost from open wounds. The thaw that comes from the oven. You turn the pie plate in your hand, trimming the edge of the crust. Bluestem & cordgrass up again. Pieces of the tribal voice howling like one.

WHITE WORDS YOU CAN HARDLY SEE AGAINST THE SKY

I travel as if at the end of the world the whole tribe crosses the sky while I'm left in the burning cornfield. Or if at death, when the spirit walks to the window & out across the yard leaving the bones under the quilt in bed. The pattern made with old dress-scraps while the days I wore them have skipped. That dress with the red button missing I sewed with blue thread. You know there are times we are not ourselves but joined as a maple leaf again to the tree. Imagine tying it back with thread from the tin box on the shelf. & you think of the world inflated as a knuckle-bone half-buried in the flesh of your hand. The marble in the museum dug from some yard in Indian Territory. As if a farm-pond were taken out of the dirt & another were put on top of it, upside down, surface to surface without spilling! That's a circle! The moon round as the face of a warrior who sees the Great Spirit. NO! The whole head.

PORTRAIT OF THE DISGUISE ARTIST

I reach down into the box, clasp my hand under his buttocks to hold him up. Not an infant, nor a wounded bird, but the thought of my Great-great-grandfather. Outside the wind heaves loose snow along the road. I hear it hiss like the furnace. I pack the box with frozen grass, dirt-clods still in the roots. The thermometer squats on zero. The frost travels the frozen window like the swollen feet of Cherokees. I hear them when winter scrapes the raw nerve in the spirit. Great-great-grandfather falls through the frozen river. I don't know if he can find his way back. I jerk him toward the surface. Now he paws the air. I dry him off, bury him under the grasses in the box until he thaws. The cold is an evil spirit. I feel it on my back. Great-great-grandfather's ghost still walks the frozen path to Indian Territory. The cold warps his bones, the skin parts in tiny cracks, the blood like red birds on the bony branches of the bush. How does anyone survive? Fly to the new territory, I say. Grow strong. His wings caked as though a blanket of frost on his back. His squawks seeping into mine.

KEMO SABE

In my dream I take
the white man
slap him
til he loves me.
I tie him to the house
take his land
& buffalo.
I put other words
into his mouth
words he doesn't understand
like spoonfuls
of smashed lima beans
until his cheeks
bulge.
Chew now, dear
I say.
I flick his throat
until he swallows.
He works all day
never leaves the house.
The floors shine
the sheets are starched.
He wipes grime
from the windows
until clouds dance
across the glass.
He feeds me
when I'm hungry.
I can leave whenever
I want.
Let him struggle
for his dignity
this time
let *him* remember
my name.

PORTRAIT OF THE ARTIST AS INDIAN

She severs the buffalo hide down the backbone
pulls the skin to the belly.
She separates the muscles, knifes along the grain.

She lifts the white flower-patches of fat to her nose
licks the blood from the wound in the hide.
She slices into the hot belly
loosens the pouches, vessels, the stomach,
bladder, the bands that hold them.

Now she scrapes the skull, pulls the teeth,
stretches the meat on sticks to hang on the drying line.

The ribs like rungs of a rocker the wagons carry
across the land.
She dismantles the carcass
the way old stories are carried into the heart.

The entrails washed at the creek,
the hide tanned.

Finally a medicine pouch sewn from 2 little tufts
of the ears.

LONE DOG

The frozen land thaws & leaves puddles in the ears. Lone Dog marks the missiles that whiz into the air like a roar of gnats around his peaches. He makes a marble of the earth. The comets & meteors hiss past him in space. Here in the hunting grounds the buffalo herds transferred from earth. The Indians transfigured. See the warriors loose from their pens. It's nothing to die. One is simply flicked off. They hold their umbrellas over their heads. Their Hudson Bay coats marked with the price of 4 beavers. Lone Dog draws the flesh around his fingernails again, covering the old fire that burned his hands, the stubs of his fingers, the white tubes of bones running up his arms. He draws his painted rawhide parfleche hanging on a rope of braided buffalo beard. The fringe ripples as if still in the gash of winter wind. He draws his breastplate of hair-pipes, blanket-leggings, & the stuffed skin of a kingfisher in his hair so he can ride swiftly into battle. It's a Power that came to him in fasting. His braids are wrapped in otter skin. He draws his flintlock & shield. His horse's tail tied up for battle & its ears notched. He draws himself riding across the plains again. He starts once more into battle.

THE IMAGINARY INDIAN

He looks at his winter count his whirlwind of time.
He knows the ages pass roughly as a rockslide

Where was he since the 1st water he came from?
Is not the eardrum a spiral shell?
Do not words still crawl to dry ground?

Lone Dog knows the winter count starts with death
then spirals outward from the core.

He traces pictographs of furry horses dirt lodges
the lost buffalo tracks.

Lone Dog knows afterwards
warriors chase beavers the squirrel wild turkey.
The spotted horses with "hail" war paint.

He knows afterwards the faceless warriors hang beaver-
tails on their scalp-shirts.

He follows with his finger the black moon
the exploding sun.

. . . the people of this lande have no kynge nor lorde nor
theyr god [.] But all thinges is comune / this people
goeth all naked But the men & women have on theyr
heed / necke / Armes / Knees / & fete all with feders
bounden for there bewtynes & sayrenes. These folk lyven
lyke bestes without any resonablenes & the wymen be
also as comon. & the men hath conversacyon with the
wymen / who that they ben or who they fyrst mete / is
she his sister / his mother / his daughter / or any other
kyndred. & the wymen be very hotte & dysposed to
lecherdnes. & they ete also on[e] another [.] The man
eteth his wyfe [,] his chylderne / as we also
have seen & they hange also the bodyes or   VI
persons fleeshe in the smoke / as men do with
swynes fleshe. & that lande is ryght full of
folke / for they lyve commonly. iii. C. [300] yere & more
with sykeness they dye nat / they take much fysshe for
they can goen under the water & fe[t]che the fisshes
out. & they werre also on[e] upon a nother / for the
olde men brynge the yonge men therto / that they gather
a great company therto of towne partyes / &comme the
on[e] ayene the other to the felde of bateyll / & flee on[e]
the other with great hepes. & nowe holdeth the fylde /
they take the other prysoners & they brynge them to
deth & ete them / & as the dede is eten then sley they
the rest. & they been eten also / or otherwyse lyve they
longer tymes & many yeres more than other people for
they have spyces & rotes / where they them selfe recover
with / & hele them as they be seke.
—from a Dutch pamphlet between 1511 & 1522

DEATH CRY FOR THE LANGUAGE

Grandmother

tuya:taht'a'	branches at the top
ti:yawhi:t.la	land lizard
huni:kawheh'	they saw
ah:kwahi:'	big
i:kit'a	size
atsi:laha	all afire
diti:k'a'nheh'	he was looking at us
na'yaha'	all rocks
awtali'	over big mountains

Her Daughter

On that cold morning in the boarding school
they lined up the language to be shot
the air was hard against us
we heard the guns
watched the words fall
there was no-light from the sun.

The Granddaughter

I lived on the edge of town
NEARLY A YEAR
TWICE the wind touched down
ripped husks from corn
roofs from a house & shed
Sometimes the wind is GRAVITY
I feel it lift
when I walk down the road
Other times of course
it's got a hand like my Father
but IT'S THE ROCKS
that hold the house down
the way memory HOLDS—
so that NOT ANYTHING
the green sky gives can matter.

Grandmother

Grandpa & Grandma left Georgia in the old country,
some came from North Carolina, the old country too.
Mamma was a girl then. The Soldiers drove um out.
They didn't want to come. Soldiers said go or
they'd kill. They'd stick bayonets in um. Some got
pots, dishes, skillet, clothes, yuh, bed clothes
too. I've got the dish Grandma brought. I eat
beans out um. But some came with nothing, not
shoes, not blanket. Next day Soldiers drove um
west. 1st day easy. Grandma said Soldiers felt
good. But every day got worse. Just drove um like
cattle. Grandma said she walked in snow, Grandpa
walked too. They crossed creeks to chins, lots of
mud. Crossed rivers on rafts, hollow logs. Soldiers
had wagons. Fed um 2 times some days, sometimes
feed 1. Soldiers ate all the time & took care of
horses. Lots of Cherokees were sick & died, too
weak to walk. They buried um beside the trail.
Clothes got bad, shoes too. Most clothes all gone
when they got to new country. They found lots of
trees but the land was no good in hills. The good
land *awtali'* was over the mountains in old country.
Grandma hated the Trail of Tears to *tuya:taht'a'*
Indian Territory.

Her Daughter

CO-TO-TE in his Father's Packard with the deer-
antlers on the hood. A zigzag border on the
lap robe. Half his face painted red, his hackled
tail, he STRUTS— TOM TOM TOM TOM. HEY EY EY EY.
The woodlands singers. POW-WOW DRUMS. The sky's
face painted half-green. Some of them came to land
with oil sleeping under it. Ho HA! The oil rights
buy them shiny beads.

The Granddaughter

Grandma had a scar on her face.
ATSI:LAHA was her old name (all afire).
Her braids crawled in the cookfire

& the FLAMES climbed to her face.
Sometimes in the wind
I smell her burnt hair & flesh.
She kept a small Rock under her bed
her Grandpa carried from Georgia.
A papoose SCREAMING at her side.

Grandmother

N'YU'NUWI (stone coat-on)
I have a small Rock my Grandpa brought from Old
Territory. It's from STONE COAT. Long ago he lived
among our people. He was a wicked CANNIBAL monster
covered with scaly armor. He went from place to
place where people did not suspect him. Sometimes
he was invisible— killing um for his food. If he
came he killed & ate everyone & there was ONLY 1 way
to save the people— He COULD NOT look on menstrual
women— If they found 7 to stand in his way the
sight would kill him. So the Medicine Man ordered 7
women to strip & stand along the path where STONE
COAT came. Soon they heard NA'YU'NUWI through the
woods. He came along the trail where the 1st woman
stood & soon he saw her he said *Yu!* grandchild in
BAD state! He hurried past but soon came to the
next & cried again *Yu!* my child in terrible way! He
hurried past her but now he VOMITED blood. He met
3rd & 4th & 5th & 6th woman each one his step grew weaker
until when came to last from whom sickness had
just begun— NOW BLOOD poured from his mouth & he
FELL on the trail. Then the Medicine Man drove 7
stakes in his body & pinned him to the ground. When
night came they piled logs over him & set fire to
him & all the people gathered. NA'YU'NUWI was
ADA'WE-HI Holy Man & told MEDICINE SONGS for
Healing. At midNight he sang the Hunting Songs for
calling bear & deer & turkey & animals of the woods
& mountains. As the blaze grew hotter the voice of
NA'YU'NUWI sank lower until by daylight the logs
were a heap of white ashes & his voice was still.
Then the Medicine Man raked off the ashes & there
was red *WA'DI* paint for face for hunting &
U'LUNSU'TI (magic stones)!

Her Daughter

It was easier for the women I guess. There was
always supper to get on the table. The men were the
ones wiped out. They didn't know what to do. The
new land couldn't be farmed. They lost their
Spirit. Their will to plow & raise animals. When
there's nothing to do you lose yourself in drink.
My mother's 1st husband was dead before he died. He
left her with several small children to raise. All
the talk about the Spirit & I never knew what it
was. Other men came around. They lived off her for
a while. We always got supper to get on the table.

The Granddaughter

I take the Rocks with me
no matter where I live.
I think 1 year I lived
5 different places.
I move in & get my Rocks settled
then I feel the Spirit move on
& I follow.
Or I move in with someone
& it doesn't work out.
1 house I lived in I knew
something bad had happened
on the land.
Whoever helps me move
(though I can do it myself)
says what's that box of Rocks?
Now sometimes
I put them in other boxes
so one is not so heavy
& put a blanket on top

Grandmother

ye ye
in old beaver-hunting ceremony
Dancers circle with shuffling step
they carry a stick on their shoulder like a gun
DAWN:HI:LI (going to hit with something)
they hold the stick in their left hand

strike dead beaver in the circle
Dancers cry *HYU HYU*
the beaver JERKS when Dancers strike
TAWY TAWYI YO'HYO! Stone Coat Hunting Song.

Her Daughter

Well, he cleared his throat
a fat-bellied man in high-heeled boots
his ponytail down his back
I'm Co-To-Te's son (cough)
I went to a pow wow last year
& everything went wrong
(step back, look away)
A man died— maybe heart attack
or the heat
Then a car caught fire & burned
just like a house
2 tribes got in a fight (cough)
(song about pow wow)
I was in prison
(step back, look away)
not much difference (cough)
from the boarding school
(people laugh)
only they don't kill you as fast
in the school (clear throat)
(people laugh)
I'm on my way if I can make it
somewhere in Kentucky (cough)
they're digging up old burial grounds
stealing face masks
(step back, look away)
if you know the spirits you know
you can't disturb the dead
(step back, cough, look away)
or you & your family are in danger
We're going to sing songs
about the digging up
(cough, look away)
I got 25 years to serve in Ohio
(sing prison song)

the priest said peace on you
a little boy who could hardly talk
said peece on you father
(people laugh)
I can't tell the other jokes I know
(song about love)
I think I'm in love
yeah yeah yeah

The Granddaughter

Most people don't believe in animal transformations
anymore, but the other night, I, the OWL— HOOTED IN
THE OAK. —WHO WHO WHO *HI:YATSITU'HI:HI:'YO.* The
night was full of dark bugs, flying spirits, really,
I sat in the tree— I heard Grandmother talk—
She spoke so softly I could hardly hear her. It
was as though IF I turned her up, I'd hear there was
NOTHING there. That's the terrible secret I have
to keep— WHO WHO WHO!!!!

Grandmother

I whisper because it's wrong to speak.
My throat-hurt from swallowing words,
my neck-swell as if I wear goiter *tuya:taht'a'*
                                    ti:yawhi:t.la
                                    huni:kawheh'
                                    ah:kwahi:'
                                    atsi:laha
                                    diti:k'a'nheh'
                                    ha'yaha'
                                    awtali'
Our land back east over Rocky Mountains.
But lizard took it & marched us to woods of Indian
Territory. We had visions of big fire.
They say it is army marching through our old lands.

Her Daughter

The QuiVerEE. ZEET! ZEET! The little clawed feet
of the turkeys DANZE. I MoUrn for Co-To-Te. The
warriors we lost. The land that sank with tHEM.

When you take a man's language, you take his meaning.
Acht! That's the bang of it at sunrise. The firing
squad of light. The quibble-ree. Your words rush
out of you like dust from a mop in the prairie wind.
You see yourself fly— Blown far away without a
chance of getting back, no matter what— The truth
is— without words, you're a ghost of yourself
hanging on.

The Granddaughter

I count my Rocks every day.
That one with Spirits coming out—
The other black as night
(it was CoaL from kenTucky).
I have a Rock with a white line
_____ like a falling comeT.
A smooth Stone from the tongue of a creek.
SpoTTed Rock.
RockET.
Fozzil Rock with a wing.
Flat ROck.
RocK with the swirl of a wind-cloud that touched down TWICE
while I lived in that house—
But the Rocks held the floor down.
NOW I Dance in my leg-rattles around the fire.
WHO WHOOOOOOOO!!
Moon RoCk like my Grandmother's scar.
Sometimes I hold a rock
& think I hear old voices.

Grandmother

In the Boarding School for Indian girls, the oil
lantern was a campfire on the table at night.
Shadows flickered the wall where animals prowled.
Some girls died with smallpox. Others screamed when
they saw their faces. At night I felt the old burn
on my cheek & sang the Medicine Song. I watched the
Ancestors rise in half-sleep— Warriors strutted
across the pitted face of moon— Chanting against
sickness.

Her Daughter

The moon slants back into the corridor of that old
boarding school. I could believe in transfer again—
standing in the line for vaccination, my legs
quivering like a rabbit's. The slick floors & bare
walls. Nothing to hold on to but air. My mouth
tasted coppery. We all cried. Afterwards the hard
wind blew all night— Windows clucked like hens.
Soon I saw the 1st round black moon high on my arm.
Later the paler one under it.

The Granddaughter

I'd sneak out the window at night.
The screen was torn anyway.
They never knew I was gone.
Hitchhike into town with anyone who passed.
I marked my year with drunkenness & arrest.
I had a friend—
sometimes we—
well, she knew a man
a veteran in a wheelchair
with an American flag over his lap.
We'd dance for him without our clothes.
He'd howl old hunting songs   *HYU HYU*
& we let him—
Well —he could make us—
with—
& then she'd—

Grandmother

Acht. He sat in the boarding school & watched us
like a lizard. *diti:k'a'nheh*
If we said 1 word in Cherokee we had to chew
a bitter leaf. It made some
vomit. But at night in sleep, Ancestors
rubbed our stomachs,
gave us old food of our Language.

Her Daughter

We came to Indian Territory 3 generations ago— my
Great-grandma & Great-grandpa— My Grandma was a
girl when she came. *HEY EY EY EY.* Where are the
noises our Grandfathers made?

The Granddaughter

I loved a boy too. But my Mother didn't like him.
She sat on the porch when he came to our house &
scratched her crotch. But I went with him. Then he
married someone else. But I couldn't settle on
anything then, slept with his friends. Once he
wrapped the label from the neck of a whiskey bottle
around my toes. The girls would talk about getting
fucked. —The back seat of a car, the creek— what
else did we have to talk about— The history of our
territory as a concept of mind?

Grandmother

ta'su'yah   (we are) scratching spreading leaves
ta'su'yah
ta'su'yah
ta'su'yah
tak tak   (turkey voice)
tak tak tak tak
tak'lu   (turkey gobble)
tak'lu

In woods the Grandfathers hide under a thick mat
of moss. They cut eyeholes in their cover &
fasten chestnut leaves for ears of the wildcat.
Under moss, the Grandfathers wear woodchuck masks
with deer-tails for ear-tufts. They crawl along
the ground with magic of the wildcat, nearing
turkeys where they hide. The Grandfathers blow
their leg-bone-of-the-bird whistle. *ta'su'yah*
tak tak. They mighty hunters of turkeys where
they hide.

Her Daughter

Co-To-Te was mutilated with 2 other Indians on State
Road 3. I knew somewhere, far away, he took a
white-face mask, danced in the backyard of space.
Red rings around his eyes— A rooster jerking his
comb & wattle. He sweeps the stubbled dirt. Nearby
a boy drums his head with a stick, opening his mouth
for hollow sounds. Now a girl pulls her arms into
her sleeves. Co-To-Te spills black pocketsfull of
seed for them. The side-dancers chant *to ho to ho.*
Co-To-Te taps his clawed feet. The children gather
the seeds for the green & half-red earth in their
heads somewhere.

The Granddaughter

4 generations ago we came to the New Territory which
was later Oklahoma. My Great-Great-Grandma &
Great-Great-Grandpa. Great-Grandma was a girl when
she came. Now I am left with hollow words which
have no meaning. *Hi:yatsitu'hi:hi:'yo.*
Rifle-barrel
whiskey-bottle
closed-off throat—
The narrow passages from this world.

VII

PORTRAIT OF THE LONE SURVIVOR

I used to throw snowballs at this girl who lived by my Grandmother's house. I came out in my army surplus parka & cap with ear flaps & waited for her, stomping my feet sometimes while I stood behind the bush. If the dog barked, I dirt-clodded him. While I waited sometimes I wrapped a rock in the snowball. Then sometimes the woman across the street would call my Grandmother & tell her I was after Azalea again. Grandma yanked the hood of my parka & shut me in the pantry. When she slept I crawled thru the window that tried to let light into her dark kitchen with its water pump on the sink & the swaying ceiling. I guess it was all her boys that slept upstairs. Herbert & Henry & my father, Roose, all jumping up & down & wrestling each other to the floor & falling out of bed & dive-bombing from the chest of drawers. She cried sometimes & didn't know what came over me after all she'd done. She sat at the north window in her house with her white cat Georgia & waited for the mailman who never brought her anything. I buttoned the cap with ear flaps & dug in the snow with my stick. I thought of the places I would go. Anywhere but there. Then suddenly Whamm there was Azalea & WHAMM * I hit her. The pink angora hat & her mittens flying!! I sat in the pantry with my finger in the boysenberry jam, Grandma's canning jars lined up on the shelves like snowballs.

I try. I am trying. I was trying. I will try. I shall in the meantime try. I sometimes have tried. I shall still by that time be trying.

My father gets me in the afternoon. We stop at Varnell's & he jokes with Henry & his friends. I see the dent in the door of his pickup. On the road, he barely makes a curve. The brush jumps above the impact of a rock on the windshield * then the long crack across the glass. On the way to the rodeo, Roose passes a long row of cars. *ogi-do-da*. He laughs in his Cherokee language when I scream.

I hope when Paw-naw comes, she crashes & the relish she makes spills on the road, little bits of glass in tires & feet. I hope Paw-naw falls out of bed & the planets wobble in orbit. I hope I get sick & Georgia, the cat, gets in a fight, her ears hanging like flaps on an old pilot's helmet. I hope Cousin Flunella's spleen swells again & pooches like the weak place in Grandma's tire. I hope

Henry's infection keeps him home. All the sweat & vomit & violent fever-dreams, shoes that were all polished shit-on. I hope the house burns down. I'm going to stare into the blueberry eye of the neighbor's half-blind dog. I hope Paw-naw limps when she gets old & gets Alzheimer's disease. I hope the Christmas tree falls over this year & the turkey, cranberry jelly & Grandma's pickles rot before we eat them. I hope someone breaks into Henry's house again while he's gone. His car in the yard. I hope someone siphons out the gas.

She calls my name in class & my heart pumps my throat. I feel Roose pound me under the covers. I feel the heat race thru my hands. My head whacks an ax chopping a totem pole. She calls my name in class & her voice is a rock whamming my head. I feel chained to the backyard like the dog I pass on the way to school. Then Roose's pickup races at me & I stand in the road watching the headlights swallow me until the fierce roar passes. She calls my name in class & I am a pulsing star. A flag flapping on its pole above the schoolyard. I try to hide behind the desk but she stands over me. I feel the whack of Grandma's stick. The choke-collar on the dog. She is the bear in my nightmares whose teeth drip with saliva at my flesh. She tears bone & sinew, shredding vocal cords until I can't talk.

I see Roose in front of the liquor store. He asks a man for money. I think I will get a grocery cart from Dabner's & push it down the alley. I'll rattle thru trash cans for bottles with a ½ swallow of gin or whiskey, sleep on the park bench & stumble on the curb when I cross the street. I'll slobber as we talk about the visions of the Grandfathers, their bravery on the Trail to the New Territory. I will tell him how Grandma survives. We'll spit & urinate on the town square of Tahlequah, Oklahoma. We'll dry out gladly in the jail.

ogi:do:da / galv:la?di / he:hi / galv:ghw(o)di:yu / ge:se:sdi / winiga:-
hl(i)sda / hada:n(v)dhesgv:i / e:lohi / galv:la?di / tsiniga:hl(i)sdi:ha /
o:gahl(i)sda:y(v)di / dago:dagwisvi:i / sgiyane:hlvsge:sdi / itsv:sganv:-
tshelv:i / sgi:yago:li:gi / tsideo:tsido:li:gi / dogi:sganv:tshe:hi / a:le /
dhle:sdi / udale:na:sdi:yi / widi:sgiya:dhinv:sdanv:gi / tsatse:li:yehno
/ tsa:hlini:gidi / ge:sv:i / a:le / etsalv:ghw:(o)di:yu / nigo:hilv:i / na:-
shigwo / winiga:hl(i)sda. Our Father / above / who dwellest / honored / be / thy name. / Let happen / what thou wilt / on earth / above / as does happen. / Our food / day by day / bestow upon

us. / In that we have transgressed against thee / pity us / as we pity / those who transgress against us. / & / do not / place of straying / lead us into. / For thine is / thou strong / the being / & / thou honored / forever. This / let be.

Roose thrashes under the strap that holds him. The medicine men nail a cow-skull over his bed. They burn cedar & chant. I would pack if I could go with him. Unzip my skin from my bones. Wear my pow wow buckskin. Leave thru the crack in the ceiling where the soul passes. Roose stops breathing I stand to my feet & he starts again. That's how it will be. He'll stomp out the back door, leaving the screen to bang. It's not a great journey to the stars. I see the blueness of his feet & fingers. Part of him is gone already. His eyes closed, sometimes he calls her name as if waiting for the lift in the hotel lobby she had just taken. Sometimes he thrashes again as though still war-dancing in the rodeo arena.

I sit in the grasses at his grave. I name this day Holy. I walk back to the house thru the cockleburs that tear my legs. I will remember *ogi:do:da*. Who creates unless he has a vacuum to fill? A white crayon on white paper. A snowfleck in the sky. Who thinks of justice unless he knows injustice? Georgia sits on my lap under a corner of the white shawl. Her owl-eye looks from the window at birds in the wisteria. I think what we do matters. I tell her this & her ear flicks the shawl-edge. I stroke her old fur. She holds her paw over my knee. If the house were burning, yes, I'd take the back of her neck in my teeth & climb thru the pantry window.

UNTITLED

The sky is crisscrossed with salmon clouds. Across the road, to the north, a yard-light shines behind the white farmhouse & in the melted snow in the low place in the field. I stand looking out the window. I do not think if I am happy. It doesn't matter. All I ask is this place to work. Now the clouds are covered with dark. To the west, the last of the sky reddens between the barn & outbuildings like the band on a trout. The slow wind seems to come from all directions. I think now I have to grope within myself for the low hanging branches, the netting of clouds I can no longer see, the wire roof of the pen where the dogs howl. I finger the memory of the hunting-blinds, the bait box & lures. What do they have, holding their nothing out? At this moment any hope endures, the one deep inside, & the past, which is a long story of a washout, the overland march, the loss of all we had. The dark engulfs the sky. Now the wind is up. I hear the roar of it in the trees. In this house by myself I have always been here. In the self from which nothing can be taken.

I have 2 room House & have find [fine]
fruit every year. Peaches apples cherries
Grapes. Now at present I lived at my

VIII

own land farmer every year I have all
kinds of different fruits sell, & put away for winter
used. I have 4 head of Horse 2 room house & a stable.
For many years I am farming every year at present time
working out to make a living & support my wife, &
wood to hauled in town . . .
But now I have no Imlp [implements] to work with now.
I go around borrowed them among different Indians just
[such] as plow cultivator lister [a special plow] Gold
devil [go-devil—a sled for logs] . . . I have nothing to go
a head & work with I work hard try to make a living, at
the same time I am getting poor . . . It looks I can not
get started my wife & I both work out at all times . . . I
wante you to help me some way in regard about Imlp
tools to work with every summer.
—Cohoe, *A Cheyenne Sketchbook*, 1910

PORTRAIT OF THE SUFFICIENCY OF WINTER

Fenceposts mark a trail across the land.
Harvester, baler, combine
under snow.
The witchy trees letting the stars shine through them.
Behind the manure pile
a string of hayrolls,
the blue swollen landscape.
The air itself is frozen against the window.
uni:hlana:hi
Great Spirit
I work with a coat hanger to get into the car.
I think we're not on our own here.
The spirits strain with the pulley
hooked to the bale of sun.
It will burn when the clouds move on.
Then we'll get to the locked reason under snow.
Meanwhile there's another storm
whipping a comet's tail against the dark pines.
But under the hayrolls & manure piles
the ground remembers.
Somewhere the soft green grass unwraps the bolt,
pokes its warm air in
like the sharp point of a hanger.

PORTRAIT OF LONE DOG

You have to understand an Indian
to see he isn't there
the heavy canvas the blue seizure
of all that could go into it. Not the brush
beside the road touching down here & there
pushing a yellow house onto the hill
the leaves covering space.
Only the frame of his face
where the cavalry still moves in a corner
of his mouth. The wagons behind them.
All still. This waiting the weather out.
The men on the loading dock won't look.
No the blue, yellow blur is a gesture
committed to rage. Otherwise
Lone Dog could hunt buffalo on his tipi hide.
Now he wears a nakedness without the body
the war paint squeezed on hopeless walls
the eyes in some other land.

FEBRUARY 10, LATE AFTERNOON

These little wet trees
what are they standing along the road for?
With their spiny arms
in old brown overcoats
what do they want?
Get back.
You there with those russet leaves
still stuck to your head
don't you know cars pass here?
In the rain yet
maybe turning to ice
what do you know
gaping at the road all day?
Your only way out
is on the back of a lumber truck.
I'm in a hurry from Tahlequah to Stilwell
down steep Eldon Hill
where the guardrail's torn away
& back again
before the ice turns to snow
& I get wiped out
& sit in a ditch crying not knowing
what to do.
Is all of life this barely making it through?

LATE WINTER

for Eleanor Wilner

It's easier to gnaw through bone
than the hide of the heart.
Substance quickly takes its leave
with the flight of birds
through a field.
But memory— Ah, the longing
after it. You send
doily lace on red paper
not letting anything
guard your pasty hands.

In the cornrows all is dead-looking
but over the barn,
the entrapment of stars,
or the moon floating in its
patrol boat.
You have less hope
than an animal in a trap.

You read the scrawl of words
over the red heat of the furnace.
You let yourself go
shooting these love-hot messages
into snowbound fields
that rise upon themselves
then turn back under their covers.

Blackbirds scurry over distant air,
impatient,
trimming trees with ravings
of your raucous heart.

AFTER THE THAW

The fields are now where you can't go out into them.
The mud would fill your knees, the bottomlessness
would drown your bones. You should allow
the sun a chance to harden the muck, holding
the nostrils of clouds. You can't go
without bringing part of the land back:
The Indian tribes who camped there, the birds'
tracks in mud. A covered-wagon rocking like a sheep
just back into the field. Who can be wrong
as often as right? The harvester, hopper,
the grain-auger with its mantis-arm raised to the horizon.
Later it will spit cobs in the truck, the chaff flying high
in the air. But now fields are puckered with mud.
The barns, houses, seem to move, the trees,
the sky not tied to the land.
Old cornstalks, chopped off at the ground,
spread their root-threads like tent stakes.

THE PACK-UP

The sun, which used to set behind the barn,
now wedges itself between the next farmhouse
& first fir in the yard.
Later & later into the north
as if stopping at the shed or well for radiator water,
back to its old traveling job,
town to town,
burning off winter,
leaving a progeny of cornstalks peeping out of the ground.

It's the end of the day,
the sun plump as a chinaberry
strikes the last of the sky,
the road & green wagon with yellow wheels.
Now the old moon of the yard light
seeps its white light into the air—
Across the dip in the land
the traffic's inconsistent hum.
All day the certainty of trucks, carriers,
the squirrels digging nuts hidden in the yard,
the sheep rummaging the field
loading what they can.

ti:ki:tihu'i (where is my town or settlement?)

I hear him at night. The stray cat that roams the field longing to come in from his wandering. Longing to have a place, a tame hand stroke him. Maybe eat from a bowl. He was once someone's. I hear him call for them. He is not afraid, but looks at me with eyes that see only what they once did. I see the fur bitten away from his hind leg, an eye going bad. What does he do in the field all day? What do the ghosts of the ancestors do? The remnant buffalo? —but gather their howling & groanings, the words they carried out of this world.

PORTRAIT OF SPRING

These fields scraped off
festering with barns & silos
the pus of white farmhouses
old tribes disc-harrowed
into the ground
Now the trees full of leaves again
a rush at dawn
their green feet & hands
Craters of horses in the fields
The stars staked to the silo
Behind the barn
the moon, jelly-like
over the trough.

A GESTURE TO THE SKY

Great Spirit bless these fields
where separation becomes stalk
& kernels hide beneath the husks.
Give the little fields their crop
as if yellow buffalo on stilts.
Let the stalks wave
their arms loose in the wind,
the movement when empty space
is pushed away
& hot wind braids the tassels
of these chambered cobs
these cliff dwellings in a field.

JUST AFTER

You would think these tiny green rows on fields
would never be cornstalks hiding the next farm.

But you let yourself go when you're in an empty place
& there's nothing else to do.

You know the runny strings of corn jump higher
out of the ground just after rain.

You know that over all the stars
the pressure pushing outward from the core
the gravity pulling inward

until the stars grow brighter (wow).

You see a collapsing star
a nebula the shape of Lone Dog

pointing out the cloud-swirl & whirlwinds over the earth
the whole galaxy itself the shape of his winter count!
A power sign he knows it now.

You see the stellar corpse the black hole of his history
his light pulled through to the other side.

You rejoice in his universe
the dream hearing afterward the shape of it

now holding wisdom from the local group
way down here in glory.

Notes

The CALENDAR of the DAKOTA NATION
embracing the period from 1799 to 1870. inclusive.

LONE DOG'S WINTER COUNT

A winter count is the recording of one event to mark the year. Since years are reckoned by winters, the calendar is called a winter count. Instead of a winter with a number—1800–01, for instance—each year has a pictograph. 1800–01 in the center of the count looks like a bamboo fence, but it marks the thirty Dakotas killed that winter by Crow Indians.

Lone Dog, a Yankton Dakota, who drew his chronicles in a spiral shape on a buffalo robe, is probably best known. Winter counts aren't that numerous anyway. Mainly recent history and mainly the Dakota tribe in the northern plains where the last of the Indian wars took place.

The spiral shape of the winter count is a mystery. But while sitting in the planetarium in Chicago in the summer of 1988 during a residency at the Newberry Library, I saw the spiral galaxy of the Milky Way, which is also called the Local Group, and immediately connected it to Lone Dog's winter count I had just been studying in the D'Arcy McNickle Center for the American Indian at the Newberry. The winter count seemed to be a power sign. Lone Dog was both recording the power of, and invoking the power for, the Indian culture.

I think Lone Dog was moved to keep his annals because of the demise of the Indian nation. He saw it even then. Almost every pictograph has to do with death or hunger or war or disease or some cataclysmic event, with only once in a while a plenty-buffalo-meat-winter.

Of course Lone Dog didn't have direct knowledge of the shape of our galaxy, but by instinct of the way things move, and by spirit-quest, these things are known. In the process of Lone Dog's "making," possibly starting at the buffalo's liver, the trophy for the one who killed the buffalo because of the strength it gave, and moving toward the heart, Lone Dog established the markings of the human mind on events.

Waníyetu yawápí (Winter Count)
by Shunka-ishnala (Dog Lone) Lone Dog
Yanktonai, tribe of Dakotas, near Fort Peck, Montana

1. 1800–01 Crows killed 30 Dakotas
2. 1801–02 Smallpox-used-them-up-again-winter
3. 1802–03 Dakotas-stole-American-horse-with-shoes-on
4. 1803–04 Plenty-wooly-horses-winter
5. 1804–05 Dakotas danced-calumet-dance & went-to-war
6. 1805–06 Crows came-&-killed 8 Dakotas
7. 1806–07 Ree killed while about-to-catch-Eagle while hid-in-Earth-hole-trap-with-bait
8. 1807–08 Came & killed Chief with red-shirt-on
9. 1808–09 Dakota-who-killed-Ree killed-by-Rees
10. 1809–10 Little-Beaver's-house-burned-winter
11. 1810–11 Black-Stone made Medicine with White Buffalo-Head held above Him
12. 1811–12 Dakotas fought-battle with Gros Ventres many-killed
13. 1812–13 Dakotas caught wild horses in sand hills first-hunted-horses-with-lariats
14. 1813–14 Many-Died-Blast-of-Air [Whooping Cough]
15. 1814–15 Dakotas killed Arapaho in his lodge
16. 1815–16 Sans-Arcs-made-large-dirt-lodge-winter
17. 1816–17 Plenty-buffalo-belly-winter
18. 1817–18 Dry-timber-built-trading-store-winter
19. 1818–19 Many-Died-Measles
20. 1819–20 This-time-good-timber-built-trading-store
21. 1820–21 Trader gave Two-Arrow a War-Dress for Bravery
22. 1821–22 Star-passed-by-with-loud-noise-winter
23. 1822–23 Another-trading-store-this-one-at-mouth-Little-Missouri-winter
24. 1823–24 First-White-appeared-&-Dakota-helped-attack-Ree-village-winter
25. 1824–25 Chief Swan all-horses-killed
26. 1825–26 Many-Dakotas-drowned-Missouri-River-flood-winter (squaws & children fall-through ice)
27. 1826–27 Hungry-Dakotas-ate-rotting-buffalo-died-gas-poured-from-mouth-winter
28. 1827–28 Mandan-Stabbed-Dakota-with-Knife Arm-Withered
29. 1828–29 White-Man-builds-dirt-lodge-winter
30. 1829–30 Bad-Arrow Indians killed Yanktonai Dakota
31. 1830–31 Many Crows killed Bloody-Battle
32. 1831–32 One White Man killed another
33. 1832–33 Stiff-Leg-with-war-bonnet-on-died-winter
34. 1833–34 Storm-of-stars-winter

35. 1834–35 Chief Medicine-Hide killed
36. 1835–36 Chief Lame-Deer Shot Crow Drew-Out-Shot-Again with-same-Arrow
37. 1836–37 Band's Father Died
38. 1837–38 Many-elk-killed-in-hunt-winter
39. 1838–39 Iron-Horn built dirt lodge
40. 1839–40 Dakotas killed whole-village of Shoshoni
41. 1840–41 Dakotas made-Peace with Cheyennes
42. 1841–42 Feather-in-Ear stole spotted ponies
43. 1842–43 One-Feather raised War-party against Crows
44. 1843–44 Sans Arc made Medicine to bring Buffalo
45. 1844–45 Minneconjous-built-tipis-in-pines-to-protect-against-snow-winter
46. 1845–46 Plenty-buffalo-meat-winter
47. 1846–47 Broken-Leg Died
48. 1847–48 Two-Man killed
49. 1848–49 Humpback killed
50. 1849–50 Crows-stole-horses-winter
51. 1850–51 Old-squaw-left-to-die-sought-carcass-of-buffalo-for-shelter-&-died
52. 1851–52 Peace-with-Crows-winter
53. 1852–53 The Nez-Percés came to Lone-Horn's lodge at midnight
54. 1853–54 Spanish-blankets-brought-winter
55. 1854–55 Brave-Bear killed
56. 1855–56 White-Mustache make-Peace with Dakotas
57. 1856–57 Four-Horns now Medicine-Man
58. 1857–58 Dakotas killed a Crow squaw
59. 1858–59 Lone-Horn made Medicine to bring Buffalo
60. 1859–60 Chief Big-Crow killed
61. 1860–61 Chief Elk-that-Made-You-Understand-His-Voice-While-He-Was-Walking made Medicine to bring Buffalo
62. 1861–62 Many-buffalos-their-tracks-close-to-tipis-winter
63. 1862–63 Red-Feather killed
64. 1863–64 Crows killed 8 Dakotas [Lone Dog did not say that many Indians were captured & 38 hung at Camp Lincoln]
65. 1864–65 4 Crows caught-stealing-horses tortured-to-death
66. 1865–66 Many-horses-died-for-want-of-grass-winter
67. 1866–67 Chief-Swan Died
68. 1867–68 This-flag-flies-winter
69. 1868–69 Texas cattle brought
70. 1869–70 Eclipse-of-Sun
71. 1870–71 Fort-surrounded-bullets-fly-winter

ABOUT THE AUTHOR

Diane Glancy, born in Kansas City, Missouri, of German/English and Cherokee parents, received a BA degree from the University of Missouri, an MA from Central State University in Oklahoma, and an MFA from the University of Iowa. She currently teaches Native American literature and creative writing at Macalester College in St. Paul, Minnesota.

She is the author of three previous collections of poetry (*One Age in a Dream*, 1986; *Offering*, 1988; and *Iron Woman*, 1989) and one of short stories (*Trigger Dance*, 1990). *Iron Woman* won the 1989 Capricorn Award from *The Writer's Voice* and *Trigger Dance* won the 1990 Nilon Award, sponsored by the University of Colorado and Fiction Collective Two.

In 1990 she received a National Endowment for the Arts Fellowship for Poetry, a Minnesota State Arts Board Fellowship for Poetry, a Jerome Travel Grant for Poetry, the Mid-Ohio Poetry Chapbook Prize, a National Endowment for the Humanities Summer Institute Fellowship at the Newberry Library in Chicago, a Diverse Visions Grant from Intermedia Arts Minnesota for a poetry/music collaboration with Harmonia Mundi, a Blandin Private College Fellowship for Playwriting, and the Borderlands Theatre of Tucson Award for Playwriting. In 1991 she won the Native American Prose Award from the University of Nebraska Press for a new manuscript, *Claiming Breath*.